GAR~~~ ~~~LS

BUSH'S FRINGE GOVERN- MEN†

PREFACE BY JAMES CARROLL

as published in The New York Review of Books

NEW YORK REVIEW BOOKS, NEW YORK

THIS IS A NEW YORK REVIEW BOOK

PUBLISHED BY THE NEW YORK REVIEW OF BOOKS

BUSH'S FRINGE GOVERNMENT
by Garry Wills

Copyright © 2006 by Garry Wills
Preface copyright © 2006 by James Carroll
Copyright © 2006 by NYREV, Inc.

This edition published in 2006 in the United States of America by
The New York Review of Books, 1755 Broadway, New York, NY 10019
www.nybooks.com

Book and cover design by Milton Glaser, Inc.

Library of Congress Cataloging-in-Publication Data
Wills, Garry, 1934–.
  Bush's fringe government / by Garry Wills; preface by James Carroll.
    p. cm. — (New York Review Books collections)
  ISBN 13: 978-1-59017-210-0 (alk. paper)
  ISBN 10: 1-59017-210-8 (alk. paper)
    1. Conservatism — United States. 2. United States — Politics and government —
2001. 3. Religious right — United States. 4. Catholic Church — Relations —
Evangelicalism. 5. Evangelicalism — Relations — Catholic Church. 6. Christianity
and politics — United States. I. Title. II. New York Review Books collection.
  JC573.2.U6W545 2006
  322'.10973 — dc22

                                                    2006015735

                    ISBN-10: 1-59017-210-8
                    ISBN-13: 978-1-59017-210-0
        Printed in the United States of America on acid-free paper.

                    1 3 5 7 9 10 8 6 4 2

CONTENTS

PREFACE

THE SEPARATION OF church and state is properly regarded as a sacrosanct principle of American democracy. No mere nicety of civil society, the idea goes to the root of politics in a free nation. In order for the rights of the individual to be protected, the right of individual conscience must be enshrined above all. Conscience is a matter of more than religion, but religion is centrally concerned with conscience. Therefore the only way to assure that the consciences of citizens remain unburdened by government is for government to remain religiously neutral. A government which "makes no law respecting an establishment of religion" is refraining, precisely, from imposition on the inner life of citizens. It is not that a society that keeps church and state apart cares less about what makes for good religion than, say, a theocracy, but quite the contrary. The separation is at the service of free conscience, which is the precondition of any authentic assertion of faith.

Not surprisingly, the separation of religion and politics has been as good for religion as for politics, and that shows in the vitality of diverse American faiths. Once the church, broadly defined, was forced to withdraw from the exercise of state power, its political independence became the source of an unexpected spiritual renewal. Religions in America confronted other religions, each with its own set of absolute claims.

Religions also confronted the experience of those for whom human life is satisfactorily devoid of any religious claim. Over time, religions in America underwent a practical process of mitigating absolutism, even as the absolutes of revelation continued to be affirmed. For many, pluralism was no longer regarded as a kind of mindless relativism but as a manifestation of the rich plurality of God's ways in the world.

Even that most absolute of religions, Roman Catholicism, was transformed in its understandings both of itself and of other traditions by its encounter with America. Early in the twentieth century, the Vatican condemned the heresy of "Americanism," but by the Second Vatican Council (1962–1965), under the influence of American Catholics like John Courtney Murray SJ, it was embracing the American idea— especially the primacy of freely exercised conscience. The Vatican II declaration *Dignitatis Humanae* ("On the Dignity of the Human Person") was subtitled "On the Right of the Person and of Communities to Social and Civil Freedom in Matters Religious." It does not take an expert on the Inquisition to know what a revolution this was. Once Roman Catholicism found it possible to affirm the primacy of conscience for those of other faiths (or of no faith), it was a small step to the affirmation of such personal freedom within the

Church. Catholics, too, have the dignity of human persons. America's gift to the world is an idea of political freedom, but America has given an equally precious gift to religion—the idea of religious freedom, even within religions themselves. There can be no coercing of conscience, or, if there is, the thing being coerced is no longer conscience.

Religious reactionaries hate these ideas. The most obvious case of such contempt is Osama bin Laden, whose war on America centrally targets what he takes to be the spiritual laxity that not only tolerates but promotes the various infidelities that corrupt God's order: empowerment of women, respect for Jews as Jews (including attachment to Israel), licentious living, the leveling of the hierarchy of truth. Bin Laden is dead serious in defining his conflict with the West as a religious war. And in the West, there are those who match bin Laden not only in the religious fervor with which they wage the clash of civilizations, but also in the rejection of assumptions basic to American democracy, like freedom of conscience, and the consequent commitment to pluralism. Christian (and Jewish) fundamentalists are gleefully at war with Islamic fundamentalists, yet in their fundamentalism these people are all allies, as if their radical monotheism makes them radical univocalists. They all warn, for example, that once the question "Is there more than one way to heaven?" is answered affirmatively, another question will soon appear: "What is heaven anyway?" And of course, in having such a worry, they are right.

Benedict XVI is bin Laden's polar opposite in his attitude toward violence, but the Pope's sweeping condemnation (made as recently as the eve of his election) of what he calls the "dictatorship of relativism," like his equation, when he was Cardinal Ratzinger, of pluralism and Marxism, seems to echo the attitudes of the Islamic fanatic. To bin Laden, America is the Great Satan; to the Pope, it is the world capital of the Culture of Death. America is an "apostate nation," in the phrase Garry Wills uses to define the zealots' rejection. There is, to be sure, much to criticize in American politics and culture, especially in the nation's runaway violence at home and abroad, but the critique offered by religious zealots (from bin Laden to Pope Benedict to the right-wing evangelicals and Catholics Wills speaks of here) concerns something else. America makes real and practical the abstractions of classical liberalism, centrally embodied in religious and philosophical toleration (tolerating even the intolerant), and that is what reactionaries cannot abide. As events have shown, America's toleration is an idea with wings, and not even the walls of hyperconservative societies are high enough to keep it out. America is the home base all that religious zealots hate. And however much they see themselves as patriots, that includes the American zealots, like those identified by Wills in this stirring book.

For all of the virtues of the separation of church and state, this tradition has had one profoundly negative consequence. Because matters of religion have been kept in a realm apart, the zone designated as "private," the kinds of human development fostered in the so-called public square have not found a hospitable niche in religion—or for religion. In America, the task of education has overwhelmingly belonged to the consciously nonreligious sphere, with "public schools" and institutions of higher learning without religious affiliations setting the tone and standards for education generally. For the supremely important reason that the consciences of pupils must not be even implicitly coerced by government-sponsored initiatives, all instruction in religion, as well as exercises of religion like prayer, has been banned from public classrooms. This has led to a widespread religious illiteracy, and not even those educated, whether partially or completely, by religiously affiliated "private" schools are exempt from it, since they too suffer from the corrupting dichotomy. Most "secular" Americans are too ignorant to know how this lack in their education undercuts them, while relatively few American believers have been offered significant religious instruction by their institutions of faith. The result is a population that takes for granted the methods of historical and critical thinking in all other areas of life while remaining intellectually immature when it comes to religion.

America is famously a churchgoing nation, but in those churches Americans are ill-equipped to think critically about what they are told. To cite only one charged example, Christians, during Holy Week, take the gospel accounts of the death of Jesus at the hands of "the Jews" as historical fact, continuing the "Christ-killer" tradition that is the ground of anti-Semitism. (Not only Mel Gibson thinks the Gospel of John was written by an eyewitness; so, apparently, do the legions of interviewers who were unable to challenge him on the question when his film *The Passion of the Christ* was at issue.) When religious leaders offer obviously simplistic answers to complex moral questions (from the beginning of life to the end of life), their congregants use the "wall of separation" to avoid challenging such teaching, or to be really challenged by it. If they give assent to ethical norms that seem unconnected to real experience, it is only assent to an abstraction, applying, if at all, on Sunday—the "separation" in time—not on weekdays.

To take a blatant example of this habit of mind, many Catholic politicians claim to be obediently "pro-life" in the privacy of conscience, while being "pro-choice" in the exercise of their public responsibility—as if conscience can be walled off like this. Instead of arguing, for example, that abortion is sometimes the necessary lesser of evils, such Catholics in public life claim to agree with their bishops that it is always murder, while voting to support it anyway. The moral thinking of bishops is bankrupt, but so is the moral thinking of many Catholics, even as in practice (when the unwanted pregnancy, say, is their own) they effectively dissent from the bishops' teaching.

The evangelicals' measure of religious truth is the emotional experience of being born again; the conservative Catholics' measure of religious truth is thirteenth-century Christendom. What evangelicals and conservative Catholics have in common is the conviction that religious truth (even as they measure it differently) is to be accepted, not thought about. In this, oddly, the reactionaries have a powerful ally in the American tradition of "separation." It is not only that critical thinking is absent from public religious expression in

America, but, worse, that devoted religious people regard critical thinking applied to belief as somehow sacrilegious, doubt as somehow a violation of the faith. Nonreligious people, meanwhile, have been duped into thinking that a respectful silence is the proper response to outrageous inanities whenever they come attached to religion. When George W. Bush, asked to identify his favorite political philosopher, named Jesus Christ, no reporter dared to follow up with the question "What political philosophy do you find in Jesus' life or teaching?" Bush, that is, had used religion to preempt a line of inquiry he was incapable of pursuing. It worked because the reporters were as incapable as he was.

This lacuna in the American political culture is as wide as a chasm, yet rarely addressed. The inability of the broad public, including the press, to apply normal methods of reason to religion is what accounts for George W. Bush's tremendous success in drawing energy from religion—and in drawing votes from religion, too. (It was, after all, bishops quick to excommunicate Catholics with different views who gave Bush his margin over John Kerry in 2004. Kerry is a Catholic, of course, but he is, for those bishops, the wrong kind of Catholic—the kind who takes Vatican II to heart, including its elevation of conscience.)

In this book, Garry Wills shows how everything from war-making to science to social justice has been transformed by the Bush administration's manipulations of "faith-based" appeals: war too readily launched and defined as holy; science inhibited by a fake intellectual "balance" that further undermines education while threatening the environment; public structures of social justice dismantled in favor of charities (most church-related) that are supposed to provide basic needs. Bush has wreaked this havoc in alliance with conservative evangelicals and certain like-minded Catholics who exploit him for their own purposes (in sum, to roll back the Enlightenment) as efficiently as Bush exploits them for his. But their common success, to date, has depended on the terrible American habit of leaving the critical mind at every door leading into the realm of religion. Now that religion is joined to state power in ways it has not been in this Republic, with drastic possibilities ahead, the task of challenging what Wills calls the "contact points" that make that joining possible has become urgent. Garry Wills comes to this task out of the great Catholic tradition in which faith submits to reason, in which doubt shows the way to firmer belief. Famous as a master of the critical-historical method, having applied it magnificently to the politics of America, Wills here shows how and why the politics of religion, too, must be understood, criticized—and changed.

—JAMES CARROLL

FRINGE GOVERN-MENT

As published in *The New York Review of Books*
October 6, 2005

FRINGE GOVERNMENT

THE ELECTION OF Pope Benedict XVI increases, naturally, the importance of certain conservative members of the American Catholic Church hierarchy; but it also increases the influence of some Catholics who are not bishops—who, in fact, have put pressure on the hierarchy. Four men especially had good relations with the Vatican of John Paul II and will have even closer ties to that of Benedict XVI. They are also situated at the contact points between the similar ruling systems of the Vatican and the White House, along with overlapping financial support systems. Two of these four are laymen (Michael Novak and George Weigel) and two are priests (Joseph Fessio and Richard John Neuhaus). I have just named them in the rising order of their probable importance.

Michael Novak has been a deft maneuverer up an improbably jerry-built scaffolding. He began in the 1960s as an ex-seminarian calling for an "open church" and attacking Paul VI's condemnation of contraceptives. He studied several years for a doctorate at Harvard, which he did not take— right-wingers sometimes call him "Dr. Novak," perhaps from some honorary degree or other. Then he served as an assistant professor of humanities at Stanford, where he was known as a beads-wearing "hippie prof" and wrote *A Theology for Radical Politics* (1968). As an outspoken opponent of the Vietnam War, he worked in the 1968 campaigns of Eugene McCarthy and Robert Kennedy.

In 1972, Sargent Shriver invited three young liberal Catholic writers (including Novak and me) to his house to advise him on the positions a Catholic might take in running for president. Only Novak showed interest in this project, and when Shriver ran for vice-president on the McGovern ticket, Novak became a press aide in that campaign. But earlier that year he was at loose ends, writing speeches for various politicians, including a seconding speech for George Wallace at the Democratic National Convention—an odd credential for one who would later be appointed by the Reagan administration as US ambassador to the UN Human Rights Commission.

By that time Novak had moved from the hippie left to the hard right and written *The Spirit of Democratic Capitalism* (1982). He collaborated with Nixon's rich Catholic former Secretary of the Treasury William Simon in criticizing the American bishops' 1984 pastoral letter on the failings of the US economy with regard to the poor, and he won the 1994 Templeton Award (with a cash prize of one million dollars) for the advancement of religion. He was invited to Rome by President George W. Bush's ambassador to the Vatican to defend the attack on Iraq, which the Pope had deplored and Novak had promoted along with his fellows George Weigel, Richard John Neuhaus, and Catholic fellow traveler Jean Bethke ("I am not in full communion with the Catholic Church") Elshtain.

George Weigel also climbed the foundations ladder to become president of the Ethics and Public Policy Center in Washington (1989–1996). He moved to being a fellow of the center while he wrote the most influential biography of John Paul II (*Witness to Hope*, 1999), a book that will be pivotal to the present pope's announced rush to canonize his predecessor. With good sources in Rome and Poland, Weigel has received the papal cross Pro Ecclesia et Pontifice, and he serves on the editorial board of Richard John Neuhaus's monthly magazine *First Things*, which has a circulation of 39,000.

Joseph Fessio is the present pope's man in America—he refers to him, justifiably, as "my friend Pope Benedict." Fessio studied theology at Regensburg with Professor Ratzinger, who directed his dissertation on the theologian Hans Urs von Balthazar (a favorite of John Paul as well as of Benedict). With three other Ratzinger students (two of them now cardinals) Fessio founded the Casa Balthazar study center in Rome, under the patronage of Cardinal Ratzinger. Fessio also founded Ignatius Press in America, which is Ratzinger's American publisher. When Fessio had a falling out with his Jesuit superiors at the University of San Francisco, he became the provost of the new Ave Maria University in Naples, Florida, founded with a $250 million grant from the Domino's Pizza fortune of conservative Catholic Thomas Monaghan.

Fessio, who knows how dear to Pope Benedict liturgical retrenchment is, began an institute called Oremus, to bring back Latin in the Mass, the altar faced away from the people, adoration of the Host, and Gregorian chant (all favored by then Cardinal Ratzinger). These positions move partway toward the more-papal-than-papalist Latin liturgies of Mel Gibson in his private chapel. Fessio is himself super-papalist. In a television interview, he told me that if the Catholic authorities ever changed their stand on contraception, their church would go out of business. Because of Fessio's close ties with the current pope, the author of an article on him in the UK journal *The Tablet* called Fessio "The Priest Who Bestrides America."

Richard John Neuhaus was a Lutheran pastor opposed to the Vietnam War who became a Catholic priest in 1991, after he had published *The Naked Public Square* (1984) advocating the reinjection of religion into politics. He is the founding editor of *First Things*, in every issue of which he writes an extensive summary of points he thinks relevant to the interplay of religion and politics during the month. Why do I think him the key figure in this "gang of four"? Well, for one thing, he is a favorite of Karl Rove, who would gladly talk with any of these men but who singled out Neuhaus as a helpful adviser even before Mr. Bush became president. Neuhaus was asked to come see Governor Bush, which began a long relationship. As *Time* noted in February of 2005:

When Bush met with journalists from religious publications last year, the living authority he cited most often was not a fellow evangelical, but a man he calls "Father Richard," who, he explained, "helps me articulate these religious things."

Evangelicals and Catholics Together (ECT)

Neuhaus consults with President Bush on what both men call "culture of life" issues like stem cell research. We see at last a realization of evangelicals' worst nightmare when they opposed the election of John F. Kennedy—the sight of an American priest relaying papal dogma to the ears of a president of the United States. The ironic thing is that evangelicals are now cheering Neuhaus on while he does what no priest would have dared to do in the 1960s. Neuhaus favors religious intervention in politics which far outruns anything Catholics could have envisaged in the past—as we saw in the last presidential election. Some American hierarchs, especially Archbishop Raymond Burke of St. Louis, threatened at that time to deny communion to political candidates like John Kerry, who voted for legalized abortion. Neuhaus, who is a great admirer of Cardinal Burke, applauded his position, and rebuked bishops who took a more moderate approach. In the issue of First Things appearing just a month before the 2004 election, Neuhaus accused D. C. Cardinal Theodore McCarrick of misrepresenting Cardinal Ratzinger's communication to him— of watering down a letter that supported the withholding of communion. Neuhaus predicted that McCarrick's moderation would end his chances of becoming the leader of the American hierarchy (Neuhaus's own candidate for that role is Cardinal Francis George of Chicago).

There are many ironies here. In the aftermath of the pedophile scandals in the Catholic Church, some Catholic liberals called for more initiatives from outside the hierarchy; but most of the lay and clerical activists who have taken up that assignment have been conservatives, who criticize the bishops for not being rigid enough in their decrees. A lay organization, the Cardinal Newman Society, regularly chastises bishops for not keeping abortion advocates off Catholic campuses, and Father Fessio hinted that Cardinal Mahoney of Los Angeles was not doctrinally sound on the Eucharist. The astonishing thing is that such doctrinaire old-line Catholicism is now supported by leading Protestant evangelicals—and no one is more central to this development than Neuhaus. He not only prints and praises fellow members of his Catholic "gang of four" in First Things—he welcomes conservative evangelicals like Chuck Colson, the Watergate felon turned born-again prison reformer, to his pages.

Neuhaus and Colson began in the early Nineties to develop the idea of an evangelical–Catholic coalition. This reached concrete form in a joint declaration in 1994,

"Evangelicals and Catholics Together" (a document famil-
iarly known on the religious right as ECT). Neuhaus published the eight-thousand-word text in *First Things*. Twenty
evangelicals and twenty Catholics signed it. Among the
Catholics were such influential figures as the late Cardinal
John O'Connor of New York (who ordained Neuhaus),
Cardinal (then Bishop) Francis George, Cardinal (then Fa-
ther) Avery Dulles, and (of course) Michael Novak and
George Weigel. The most prominent evangelicals, aside
from Colson, were Pat Robertson, Bill Bright (of Campus
Crusade for Christ), Richard Mouw, James J. I. Packer, and
Mark Noll.

Despite such support, ECT caused what the best report on
the document calls "a firestorm" in the evangelical camp.[1] It
was said that doctrinal divisions between the two religious
communities had been downplayed to create what was
called a "cobelligerency" on political issues like abortion
(which got the longest treatment of any practical matter in
the document). In an attempt to create deeper theological
backing for the coalition, three more documents were developed in succeeding years—ECT II on justification
(1997), ECT III on the Bible (2002), and ECT IV on the communion of saints (2003). These were so successful among

evangelicals that one of the original signers of ECT, Mark Noll, was prompted to take the documents as a harbinger of a possible "end of the Reformation."

Of course, the convergence of evangelicals and Catholics was not begun or completed by Neuhaus's ECT. Old animosities had been disappearing for many political reasons. The Protestant objection to public support for private (read: Catholic) schools was broken down by the *Brown v. Board of Education* decision. Private schools were set up in the South to avoid integration, and then religious schools developed from these to protest the ban on school prayer, the teaching of evolution, and sex education in public schools. Home schooling, religious schools, and right-wing colleges are now a principal seedbed of the religious right—as *The New Yorker* pointed out in its June 27, 2005, article on Patrick Henry College, in Purcellville, Virginia, whose students flow into congressional and White House internships.

Francis Schaeffer, the original formulator of a "co-belligerency" strategy on abortion, had also softened evangelical resistance to Catholicism.[2] When Jerry Falwell's Moral Majority made opposition to abortion its major issue, some Catholics joined his effort, even though the evangelicals used pseudo-biblical arguments and the Catholics relied on papal pronouncements. The latter point would once have spelled the end of cooperation with the Protestants; but a new urgency in the "pro-life" movement overrode past causes of division.

The quieting of old fears could be seen in the fervent outpouring of evangelical support for Mel Gibson's *The Passion of the Christ*, which was based on a book that would once have been condemned by evangelicals as "Mariolatrous." Gibson's "sedevacantist" view of the modern papacy—i.e., the belief of those Catholics who do not recognize the popes from John XXIII on—would have precluded Vatican support for his movie before the apocalyptic coalition created a *pas d'ennemi à droite* mentality among "cobelligerents." Extreme branches of both the evangelical and the Catholic communities united to promote the movie, which was a commercial "miracle." The fact that some Protestant churches required attendance at the movie looked like a strange inversion of Catholic support for the movie *The Song of Bernadette* in the 1940s.

Colson and Neuhaus came along at just the right time to solidify the evangelical–Catholic coalition. By 2004, a survey of evangelicals found that Pope John Paul II had a higher favorable rating (59 percent) than either Jerry Falwell (44 percent) or Pat Robertson (54 percent). There was even agreement between evangelicals and Catholics about ex-communicating members of their congregations for sup-porting abortion. While Archbishop Burke was advocating that in St. Louis, a Baptist minister, the Rev. Chan Chandler, drove nine Democrats out of his church in Waynesville, North Carolina.[3]

A Quiet Extremism

No one is better at fostering the sense of shared anxiety than "Father Richard." He does so with a quiet air of reasonable-ness which just makes his extremism more effective. In his 1984 book *The Naked Public Square*, he argued that the removal of religion from public life had undermined the historical identity of America. He praised evangelicals for the anger with which they recognized this fact. Liberals, he said, are theoretically impersonal and cold as they go about what he describes as "sterilizing" or "sanitizing" or "neutralizing" public discussion. The hot gospelers, by contrast, speak as people who have "experienced assault" on their values and identity. While posing as a moderator of their excesses, he feeds the fires of their outrage. By "invoking the nightmares we fear," according to Neuhaus, the religious right is returning to the theological origins of democracy (which he derives from Oliver Cromwell, of all people).

Neuhaus's tactical uses of extremism were on display in a symposium he created for First Things in 1996, a set of five commissioned articles under the overall heading "The End of Democracy? The Judicial Usurpation of Politics." Neuhaus admitted in his introduction that the symposium might be called "irresponsibly provocative and even alarmist"—and in fact it caused two members of the First Things editorial board, Gertrude Himmelfarb and Walter Berns, to withdraw their names from the masthead, in protest at what Berns described as a message "close to advocating not only civil disobedience but armed revolution."

One of the contributors to the symposium, Robert Bork, did not retract anything he said in it himself, but he criticized Neuhaus's introductory claim that Americans "have reached or are reaching the point where conscientious citizens can no longer give moral assent to the existing regime." But it is hard to see much difference between Neuhaus's words and inflammatory statements in Bork's own article—such as:

> It seems safe to say that, as our institutional arrange-
> ments now stand, the Court can never be made a legit-
> imate element of a basically democratic polity. . . . Per-
> haps an elected official will one day simply refuse to
> comply with a Supreme Court decision. That sugges-
> tion will be regarded as shocking, but it should not be.

The other articles were just as extremist. Colson called the
Roe v. *Wade* decision a "horrendous offense against God." He
said that we had probably not reached, yet, the point where
"government becomes sufficiently corrupt that a believer must
resist it," but "we are fast approaching this point." Robert P.
George asked, "Has the regime of American democracy for-
feited its legitimacy?" The answer, again, was not quite, but "the
hour is late." This essay is called "The Tyrant State." Hadley Arkes
concluded that "the courts are making the political regime un-
livable for serious Christians and Jews." Russell Hittinger argued:

> It is late in the day, and our options have dwindled.
> Either right-minded citizens will have to disobey
> orders or perhaps relinquish offices of public author-
> ity, or the new constitutional rulers will have to be
> challenged and reformed.

He said the latter course must first be tried, since "prompting the constitutional crisis is the responsible thing to do." It is significant that two of the symposium authors arguing that *Roe* v. *Wade* made the Court illegitimate, Robert George and Hadley Akens, were recruited by White House supporters to assure the religious right that Court nominee John Roberts is on their side.[4]

The illegitimacy Neuhaus and others attack is not just an aberration of the courts, or of the federal government more generally. The problem is a Godless culture, one that accepts wholesale murder in the form of abortion. The new religious right does not claim to be speaking for a moral majority. It knows it is a minority—in fact, it asks for protection of believers as a matter of minority rights.[5] Is the whole American nation illegitimate? (One of the *First Things* articles was called "A Culture Corrupted.") The *First Things* symposiasts said that the American regime is illegitimate because the Court upheld *Roe* v. *Wade*. But in June of this year a Gallup poll for CNN/*USA Today* showed that 65 percent of the American people oppose repeal of *Roe* v. *Wade*, with less than half that number (29 percent) favoring its overthrow. Earlier polls had shown a similar split.[6]

The division in the nation becomes more pronounced when

the question moves from abortion to mandatory maintenance of life support, an issue the religious right has lumped together with protection of the fetus. According to the March CBS poll, 82 percent of the American people were opposed to the intervention of Congress and the President in the Terri Schiavo case —only 13 percent of those polled thought the concern voiced for Schiavo was a sincere concern about her own good, while 74 percent said that the concern was politically motivated. On a related issue, embryonic stem cell research is supported by approximately two to one in the nation (58 percent to 31 percent). It is understandable that the evangelical–Catholic coalition would call this a "culture of death," subject to God's wrath and calling for extreme measures.

Governing from the Fringes

This presents a difficult problem. How do you govern an apostate nation? When the entire culture is corrupted, the country can only be morally governed in spite of itself. A collection of aggrieved minorities must seize the levers of power in every way possible. One must govern not from a broad consensual center but from activist fringes of morality. That has, in fact, been Karl Rove's strategy. He cultivates the extreme groups that are out of step with the broad consensus of the nation, since they supply the hard workers in primaries and general elections. Acting in accord with Rove's priorities, the President instantly flew back to Washington and got up in the middle of the night to sign the bill calling for further intervention in the Schiavo case. The fringe was calling the tune.

On stem cells, the fringe is so extreme that Chuck Colson has informed evangelicals they should not support for president Mitt Romney, the governor of Massachusetts, who is a Mormon, since Romney thinks that the inseminated ovum is not a human person (as opposed to the ovum that is "nidated," i.e., planted in the uterus). Colson believes that whenever any human semen enters any ovum God pops a soul in along with it—though almost 50 percent of the resulting "people" perish instantly by failing to achieve nidation.[7]

Bush's team has been as solicitous of the extremists here as on the Schiavo case—it commissioned the White House liaison to evangelicals, Jay Lefkowitz, to coordinate the formation of policy on stem cells.[8] President Bush had a ceremony in the White House for those who "adopt" embryos and bring them to birth (though encouraging such marginal adoption guarantees that most available embryos will be overproduced and destroyed).[9]

Senator Bill Frist invoked his medical expertise to look at some tapes of Terri Schiavo and declare her not brain-dead. Only Tom DeLay outdid him in the faith-over-science department when he said, "Terri Schiavo is not dead. She talks and she laughs, and she expresses happiness and discomfort. Terri Schiavo is not on life support."[10]

Most American administrations at least try (or pretend) to govern by compromise, to speak for "all the people." The Bush presidency has not even put on a show of doing this. It secretly meets with its business and religious supporters; it favors lobbyists who hold extreme views on education, the environment, the family, gun control, regulation of any kind. Its officials make appearances on extremist talk shows and in far-right-wing publications. On issue after issue, this administration is out of touch with the majority of the American people.

Most people favor sensible controls on guns, but the administration goes with the NRA extremists who think that any regulation of even the most exotic weapons would spell the elimination of all guns from American life. Most people are opposed to private accounts instead of Social Security, but the administration follows its free-market purists. A majority would vote to support the Geneva Conventions, but the administration secretly overrides them and then tries to cover up its actions. If the administration depended on only one set of extremists, it could not prevail over the general consensus; but it weaves together a chain of extremisms encircling the polity, each upholding the others, forming a necklace to choke the large body of citizens. Grover Norquist explained the strategy of governing by extremist groups to John Cassidy of *The New Yorker* (August 1, 2005):

> If you want the votes of people who are [simultaneously] good on guns, good on taxes, and good on faith issues, that is a very small intersection of voters. But if you say, Give me the votes of anybody who agrees with you on any of these issues, that is a much bigger section of the population.... And if you add more things, like property rights and homeschooling, you can do even better.

If religious extremism is only one large set of bodies in this fringe constellation, it is a powerful one. That is why federal agencies reject scientific reports on ecological, stem cell, contraceptive, and abortion issues. They sponsor not only faith-based social relief, but faith-based war, faith-based science, faith-based education, and faith-based medicine. Other administrations would be embarrassed by a high defense official who could say what General William ("Jerry") Boykin did of the 2000 election. Standing before a church audience in full military uniform, he said:

> Now ask yourself this. Why is this man [George W. Bush] in the White House? The majority of Americans did not vote for him. Why is he there? I tell you this morning he's in the White House because God put him there for such a time as this. God put him there to lead not only this nation but to lead the world in such a time as this.[11]

There could not be a better statement of the view that the moral minority has to prevail over the lackadaisical majority. Nor was this an isolated outburst. It is what Boykin repeated in churches and at prayer breakfasts, often with slides, doing this routine:

> Well, is he [slide of Bin Laden] the enemy? Or is this

man [slide of Saddam Hussein] the enemy? The enemy is none of these people I have showed you here. The enemy is a spiritual enemy. He's called the principality of darkness. The enemy is a guy called Satan. . . . Our spiritual enemy will only be defeated if we come against him in the name of Jesus.

He answered a boast by a Somali Muslim warlord that Allah was on his side by saying, "My God was bigger than his. I knew that my God was a real God, and his an idol." When the man was caught, he claims, he told him, "Mr. Atto, you underestimated our God."[12]

The man saying this was not some minor functionary but a key figure in the Defense Department's own intelligence unit—the one that gave us those assurances about weapons of mass destruction. There was a time when such views would lead to reprimand, if not to dismissal. When General Edwin Walker, a member of the John Birch Society, voiced its extremist views before his NATO troops in Germany, President Kennedy had him removed from his command. This caused an uproar in the right-wing community. Karl Rove would not risk such an uproar these days—Boykin was not dismissed, rebuked, or even disowned. He continues doing intelligence work for the Defense Department.

Rove knows that Neuhaus, while being more subtle about it, has the crusading spirit of Boykin. Neuhaus has endorsed Samuel Huntington's "clash of cultures" thesis, defended the historical Crusades as "probably justified warfare," and answered a caller on C-SPAN who said that Islam was an implacable enemy with the warning that we must "be very sober about the possibility that this really is the only Islam that is going to present itself on the world historical stage for the rest of this century." It is a more sophisticated form of Boykinism, and it informs the evangelical-Catholic support for the war in Iraq at a time when a majority of Americans have come to think it was a horrible mistake.

So much for faith-based war. How about faith-based science? The administration rejects scientists' findings on global warming, evolution, and contraception. It has put networks of right-wing religious bureaucrats in agencies such as the FDA, the NIH, HHS, the President's Council on Bioethics, the Advisory Committee for Reproductive Health, and the

5

National Center for Environmental Health. These officials have a coordinated agenda to oppose abortion, condom use, AIDS awareness programs, sex education not centered on abstinence, stem cell research, needle exchange programs, and the morning-after pill. Even the conservative Jeffrey Hart, a longtime editor of *National Review*, has criticized such activity:

> The Bush administration has devoted millions to faith-based organizations promoting abstinence, but in doing so [is] telling flagrant lies: that condoms fail to prevent HIV 31 percent of the time during heterosexual intercourse (3 percent is accurate); that abortion leads to sterility (elective abortion does not); that touching a person's genitals can cause pregnancy; that HIV can be spread through sweat and tears [Bill Frist would not deny this on the George Stephanopoulos show]; that a 43-day-old fetus is a "thinking person"; and that half of gay teenagers have AIDS. Some grants for faith-based programs stipulate that condoms be discussed only in connection with their failure.[13]

The Centers for Disease Control removed information about safe sex from its Internet site. Though peer-reviewed studies written by scientists from Columbia and Yale demon-strated that abstinence-only courses in public schools are ineffective, conservatives in the administration preferred a counter-paper prepared by the Heritage Foundation, which allowed for a margin of error of 10 percent, though 5 per-cent is the limit for scientific studies.[14] The FDA overruled its own scientific board's recommendation that the morning-after contraception called Plan B be made available without prescription. Bush had stacked the advisory panel with con-servatives, including W. David Hager, a gynecologist at the University of Kentucky who took public credit for killing the scientists' recommendation, saying God had used him to bring this about: "Once again, what Satan meant for evil, God turned into good."[15]

This reminds me of the way another panel was stacked with conservatives by Pope Paul VI. In 1968 a commission of Catholic experts, lay and clerical, on natural law (the only con-trolling norm on the matter) was about to reach the conclu-sion that there is no basis for the ban on "artificial" contra-ception. The Vatican rushed in new members and rigged the voting rules; yet the commission still reached the undesired result—so the Pope simply overruled the experts who were qualified on this subject.[16]

This is not the only way Vatican methods run parallel with those of Washington. Rome too is now ruled from the margins. Most Catholics hold views different from the Pope's on many matters. In a poll taken in April 2005, by CNN/*USA Today*/Gallup, Catholics in America favored women's ordination by 55 percent, and favored married priests by 63 percent. But these figures are misleading. Most of the minority siding with the Vatican is made up of older and more conservative Catholics. The future lies with those under thirty, who are far less submissive to the Vatican. The deepest survey of this sector of the community was undertaken with Lilly Endowment funds in 1997. It relied on many interviews and focus groups along with regular polling. Only 17 percent in this age group agreed with the Vatican on the exclusion of women from the priesthood, and only 27 percent on the celibate priesthood. So few of the young adults agreed with the Pope on contraception that they fell within the margin of error, making them statistically nonexistent.[17]

A Pew Research poll in April 2005 found that 38 percent of Catholics think a woman should be able to have an abortion "for any reason" (more Catholics get abortions than Protestants, according to the Alan Gutmacher Institute's polls of doctors). The numbers of Catholics saying that homosexuality is

"not wrong at all" is higher than those in the general population (39 percent to 33 percent).[18] Though Cardinal Ratzinger
advised bishops to deny communion to politicians voting for
legal abortion, a May 2004 ABC/*Washington Post* poll showed
that 72 percent of American Catholics opposed such action.
Even a majority of those opposed to abortion were against it.

How then do you govern an apostate church? From the
fringes. Like Karl Rove, the Pope has cultivated intense little extremist groups — Opus Dei, the Legionaries of Christ,
the New Catechumenate, and Communication and Liberation, well-financed, semi-secretive, ascetical, ultrapapalist.
Karol Wojtyla, as cardinal, spoke to Opus Dei groups when
he visited Rome. Joseph Ratzinger spoke to a Communication and Liberation group just before his election to the papacy. The Vatican equivalent of the executive branch has
been stocked with extreme loyalists, and debate on their
actions has been suppressed. In a 1998 *Motu Proprio* — or
document issued by the Pope on his own initiative — called
Apostolos Suos, national conferences of bishops were ordered
to pass no legislation except by unanimous vote and after
Vatican approval, reducing them to little more than rubber
stamps of the Pope, after the Second Vatican Council had in-
creased their importance.

The Vatican has adopted a literally marginal strategy. While still Cardinal Ratzinger, the current pope said that the Church may have to become smaller in order to become truer to itself. Just as the religious right in America has declared itself an embattled minority, Ratzinger said, "The word 'subculture' should not frighten us."[19] The fringe will be activated in Africa, Latin America, and Asia, about which the Vatican has a romantic notion of forming a circle of extremists—though the priest shortage is greater in these regions than in Europe and North America, the Vatican has warned against "syncretism" with other cultures, and Catholics compete with evangelicals there who have a married ministry and a nonhierarchical structure.

As nuns disappear and priests age, the Vatican's response is to become ever more extremist. Pope John Paul changed a long Catholic teaching tradition when he supported the need for life support in terminal cases. The hierarchy has changed its long acceptance of the theory of evolution as a scientific account—after being attacked by rightist Catholic groups for being too lax on the subject.[20] These are odd moves for authorities who claim they never change. The notion of infallibility has been expanded to cover things like the all-male priesthood and non-Catholic ordinations to the ministry. The use of "backdoor infallibility" has been evident in Stakhanovite beatifying and canonizing, sometimes of those with dubious and/or anti-Semitic records (Pius IX, Maximilian Kolbe, Josemaría Escrivá). John Paul even canonized a man, Juan Diego, historians say never existed.[21] Like American evangelicals drawing their recruits from the home-schooled, religious schools, and institutions like Patrick Henry College, the Vatican has converted Catholic seminaries into ultraconservative schools turning out priests at odds with their future congregations on matters like contraception and homosexuality.[22]

Superstitions like the cult of the Lady of Fatima have been inflated—then-Cardinal Ratzinger claimed that the Virgin Mary, appearing to subteen children in Portugal, predicted in 1917 the 1981 attempt on John Paul's life.[23] The old war between the Church and science has been revived. The current pope joined American evangelicals who attack Halloween by warning the world against Harry Potter. Pope John Paul performed three exorcisms, not all of them successful.[24] On the use of embryos for stem cell research, the Vatican is even more extreme than President Bush, who welcomes babies from "adopted" embryos—the Vatican teaches that in vitro fertilization is aways wrong, among other reasons because getting the necessary semen involves masturbation.[25] The Pope announced in August that he would again grant numerous indulgences (passes out of Purgatory)—a practice some had thought as obsolete as papal interdicts (the denial of sacraments to whole regimes).[26] If indulgences are back, can interdicts be far behind?

On condoms, the Pope agrees more with American evangelicals than with Catholics—though the *National Review*, not to be out-extremed, published an article defending the reversal of *Griswold v. Connecticut*, which made condom sales legal.[27] The denial of condoms to those with AIDS in Africa has led to deaths—causing more hostility to the Church, in some circles, than the pedophile scandals did. In fact, both the fringe power systems, holding together their own extremist networks, have drifted apart from or alienated the rest of the world.

The Bush administration had a world ready to cooperate in the hunt for terrorists after the attacks of September 11, but it drove them off by its unilateral obsession with brushing aside the UN investigations which had tied Saddam's hands and would have shown in time the absence of weapons of mass destruction. In a similar way, after the Second Vatican Council, Rome had world religions ready and anxious to join in the struggle with immoral practices around the world, but it blighted the ecumenical energies with things like *Dominus Jesus* (2000), the condemnation of pluralism that called other Christian faiths "gravely deficient." (General Boykin would just say, "Our God is greater than your God.")

Given the resemblances between the strategies for governing from the margins, it is easy to see how well placed is the Catholic gang of four I began with. Its members are perfectly able to serve as both the Pope's men and Rove's men, for reciprocally strengthening reasons. They are at the interface between two systems of power exercised from the fringes.

—*September 8, 2005*

NOTES

1. Mark A. Noll and Carolyn Nystrom, *Is the Reformation Over? An Evangelical Assessment of Contemporary Roman Catholicism* (Baker Academic, 2005), p. 15. The ECT series is given extensive treatment at the center of the book (pp. 151–208).

2. For the importance of Francis Schaeffer to the formation of the religious right, see Garry Wills, *Under God: Religion and American Politics* (Simon and Schuster, 1990), pp. 318–328.

3. "Church Split in Dispute Over Bush," Associated Press, May 10, 2005.

4. David D. Kirkpatrick, "A Year of Work to Sell Roberts to Conservatives," *The New York Times*, July 22, 2005.

5. Noah Feldman points out the shift of strategy by which the religious right now makes it court claims as an endangered minority—see *Divided by God: America's Church-State Problem—and What We Should Do About It* (Farrar, Straus and Giroux, 2005), pp. 206–212.

6. "Abortion and Birth Control," PollingReport.com.

7. "While We're at It," *First Things*, May 2005. Neuhaus agrees with Colson on the status of the embryo, but he said that Romney could perhaps be supported if he stayed true on other issues—though Neuhaus answered with a no the question "Is the Church of Jesus Christ of Latter-Day Saints a Christian communion?"

8. Esther Kaplan, *With God on Their Side: How Christian Fundamentalists Trampled Science, Policy, and Democracy in George Bush's White House* (New Press, 2004), p. 126.

9. Liza Mundy, "Out of the Freezer, Into the Family: The Booming, and Bizarre, Business of Embryo Adoption," *Slate*, May 31, 2005.

10. DeLay quoted by Bob Herbert, *The New York Times*, June 23, 2005.

11. William Boykin, Address to Good Shepherd Community Church in Boring, Oregon, June 2003.

12. MSNBC News, October 15, 2003.

13. Jeffrey Hart, "The Evangelical Effect," *Pittsburgh Post-Gazette*, April 17, 2005.

14. "Weird Science," *Christian Alliance for Progress*, June 20, 2005.

15. *The Washington Post*, May 12, 2005.

16. Robert McClory, *Turning Point: The Inside Story of the Papal Birth Control Commission* (Crossroad, 1995).

17. Dean R. Hoge, William D. Dinges, Sister Mary Johnson, and Juan L. Gonzales Jr., *Young Adult Catholics: Religion in the Culture of Choice* (University of Notre Dame Press, 2001), pp. 200–201. The survey devoted special attention to Latino-Americans and found them more traditional than Anglos, but only "slightly" (pp. 113–130).

18. "American Catholics in John Paul's Time," *The New York Times*, April 2, 2005. Catholic confidence in spiritual leaders, once very high, was at 19 percent.

19. John L. Allen Jr., *Cardinal Ratzinger: The Vatican's Enforcer of the Faith* (Continuum, 2000), p. 311.

20. For the attacks, see the Fatima Network, Perspective No. 426. For hierarchical backing off, see "Leading Cardinal Redefines Church's View on Evolution," *The New York Times*, July 9, 2005.

21. Lisa Sousa, Stafford Poole, and James Lockhart, *The Story of Guadalupe* (Stanford University Press, 1998).

22. Bishops now claim they are taking only candidates for the priesthood who agree with all papal teaching. Since the Lilly survey found that fewer than 5 percent or so of under-thirties agree with the teaching on contraception, the pool for new seminarians has shrunk drastically. Only half of the 5 percent, after all, are men, and only a minority of men ever want to be priests, so the pool is down to 1 percent or so. It is further decreased by some bishops' policy of not accepting gays. (A *Los Angeles Times* poll in 2003 found that 23 percent of young priests call themselves gay.) Many note how the number of priests has dwindled in recent decades. The prospects of resupply look grim under present guidelines, not only in the quantity of candidates available but in their quality. This is not a process that tends to produce creative or critical minds.

23. Joseph Cardinal Ratzinger, "Theological Commentary," The Message of Fatima, Congregation for the Doctrine of the Faith, May 13, 2000.

24. John Norton, "Pope Performs Exorcism Over Teenage Italian Girl," *Catholic News Service*, September 11, 2000.

25. Congregation for the Doctrine of the Faith, *Donum Vitae* (1987).

26. "World Briefing," *The New York Times*, August 9, 2005.

27. Robert P. George and Dave L. Tubbs, "The Bad Decision That Started It All," *National Review*, July 18, 2005.

JIMMY CARTER & THE CULTURE OF DEATH

As published in *The New York Review of Books*
February 9, 2006

JIMMY CARTER & THE CULTURE OF DEATH

IN 1972, I WAS ASKED by *New York* magazine to survey Southern re-
actions to the attempted assassination of George Wallace. On
my list of people to call was Georgia governor Jimmy Carter.
When I called his press secretary, Jody Powell (a name I had
never heard before), I was told it would be better for me to
come to Atlanta than to talk on the phone. (Powell was drum-
ming up attention for his man, with a view to his running for
president.) When I arrived there, Powell had arranged for me
to fly with Carter in his little state prop plane to Tifton, a small
South Georgia town where there was a meeting with local
sheriffs. The sheriffs were unhappy with Carter's liberal racial
policies, and Powell obviously thought it would be good for
his reputation nationally to be seen as standing up against
regional prejudice.

Carter used all his local ties to defang the critics—the
sheriffs did not openly turn against him—and I was im-
pressed. On the flight back, he said he wanted to drop off in
the town of Plains and see how his peanut business was doing
—a homey touch the press would be treated to ad nauseam
over the next two years. I do not remember any mention of

his local church while we were in Plains. In fact, I cannot re-
call that religion was brought up in all our hours together.
Perhaps he thought that was not something *New York* magazine
readers would respond to. At any rate, I was surprised when,
four years later, so much was made of his religion as he ran
for president. It began when he was asked, while visiting
Baptist friends, if he thought of himself as "born again." He
answered yes—not surprisingly, since the Gospel of John
(3:5) says that one must be born again to enter the kingdom
of heaven, and Saint Paul says that baptism is being reborn
into Christ (Romans 6:4). Reporters did not know this as a
basic belief of Christians—they treated it as an odd cult claim.

That led to his second-most-famous remark of the 1976 campaign. Carter was asked in a *Playboy* interview if he thought he
was a holier-than-thou person because he was born again. He
answered that, no, in fact he had committed lust in his heart
—again quoting the New Testament (Matthew 5:28). That
did it. For much of the Carter presidency, the line of some in
the press (and, as I know well, in the academy) was that he
was a religious nut. I followed him in the 1976 race and
heard a reporter ask Carter why he constantly brought up religion. He replied that he had made a determination never to
bring up religion in the campaign. But the reporters kept

asking him about it, and he had to answer them or be criticized for dodging the issue.

His attendance at church was not announced; we reporters had to ferret that out by ourselves. Carter is an old-fashioned Baptist, the kind that follows the lead of the great Baptist Roger Williams — that is, he is the firmest of believers in the separation of church and state. Unlike most if not all modern presidents, he never had a prayer service in the White House. His problem, back then, was not that he paraded his belief but that he believed. All this can seem quaint now when professing religion is practically a political necessity, whether one believes or not. There is now an inverse proportion between religiosity and sincerity.

Carter rightly says in *Our Endangered Values*[1] that the norms of religion and politics are different. His religion, at any rate, places its greatest priority on love, of God and one's neighbor, even to the point of self-sacrifice. But a president cannot make his nation sacrifice itself — that would be dereliction of duty. The priority of politics is justice, and love goes beyond that. But love can help one find out what is just, without equating the two. That is why none of us, even those who believe in the separation of church and state, professes a separation of morality and politics. Insofar as believers — the great majority of Americans—derive many if not most of their moral insights from their beliefs, they must mingle religion and politics, again without equating the two.

In his new book, Carter addresses religion and politics together in a way that he has not done before, because he thinks that some Americans, and especially his fellow Baptists, have equated the two in a way that contradicts traditional Baptist beliefs in the autonomy of local churches, in the opposition to domination by religious leaders, and in the fellowship of love without reliance on compulsion, political or otherwise. In 2000, these tenets were expressly renounced by the largest Baptist body, the Southern Baptist Convention, which removed a former commitment to the belief that "the sole authority for faith and practice among Baptists is Jesus Christ, whose will is revealed in the Holy Scriptures." What was being substituted, Carter writes, was "domination by all-male pastors." As a leading spokesman, W. A. Criswell, put it: "Lay leadership of the church is unbiblical when it weakens the pastor's authority as ruler of the church." The Southern Baptists, Carter laments, have become as authoritarian as their former antitype, the Roman Catholic hierarchy. The Southern Baptist Convention has severed its ancient ties with the Baptist World Alliance.

The marks of this new fundamentalism, according to Carter, are rigidity, self-righteousness, and an eagerness to use compulsion (including political compulsion). Its spokesmen are contemptuous of all who do not agree with them one hundred percent. Pat Robertson, on his 700 Club, typified the new "popes" when he proclaimed: "You say you're supposed to be nice to the Episcopalians and the Presbyterians and the Methodists and this, that, and the other thing. Nonsense. I don't have to be nice to the spirit of the Antichrist." Carter got a firsthand taste of such intolerance when the president of the Southern Baptist Convention visited him in the White House to tell him, "We are praying, Mr. President, that you will abandon secular humanism as your religion."

Such attitudes are far from the ones recommended by Jesus in the gospels as Carter has studied and taught them through the decades, and their proponents have brought similar attitudes into the political world, where a matching political fundamentalism has taken over much of the electoral process. Such dictatorial attitudes defeat the stated goals of the fundamentalists themselves. On abortion, for instance, Carter argues that a "pro-life" dogmatism defeats human life and values at many turns. Carter is opposed to abortion, as what he calls a tragedy "brought about by a combination of human

errors." But the "pro-life" forces compound rather than re-
duce the errors. The most common abortions, and the most
common reasons cited for undergoing them, are caused by
economic pressure compounded by ignorance.

Yet the anti-life movement that calls itself pro-life pro-
tects ignorance by opposing family planning, sex education, and informed use of contraceptives, tactics that not
only increase the likelihood of abortion but tragedies like
AIDS and other sexually transmitted diseases. The rigid sys-
tem of the "pro-life" movement makes poverty harsher as
well, with low minimum wages, opposition to maternity
leaves, and lack of health services and insurance. In combination, these policies make ideal conditions for promoting abortion, as one can see from the contrast with countries that do
have sex education and medical insurance. Carter writes:

> Canadian and European young people are about
> equally active sexually, but, deprived of proper sex
> education, American girls are five times as likely to
> have a baby as French girls, seven times as likely to
> have an abortion, and seventy times as likely to have
> gonorrhea as girls in the Netherlands. Also, the inci-
> dence of HIV/AIDS among American teenagers is

five times that of the same age group in Germany....
It has long been known that there are fewer abortions
in nations where prospective mothers have access to
contraceptives, the assurance that they and their
babies will have good health care, and at least
enough income to meet their basic needs.

The result of a rigid fundamentalism combined with poverty
and ignorance can be seen where the law forbids abortion:

In some predominantly Roman Catholic countries
where all abortions are illegal and few social services
are available, such as Peru, Brazil, Chile, and
Colombia, the abortion rate is fifty per thousand.
According to the World Health Organization, this is
the highest ratio of unsafe abortions [in the world].

A *New York Times* article that came out after Carter's book
appeared further confirms what he is saying: "Four million
abortions, most of them illegal, take place in Latin America
annually, the United Nations reports, and up to 5,000
women are believed to die each year from complications
from abortions."[2] This takes place in countries where

churches and schools teach abstinence as the only form of contraception—demonstrating conclusively the ineffectiveness of that kind of program.

By contrast, in the United States, where abortion is legal and sex education is broader, the abortion rate reached a twenty-four-year low during the 1990s. Yet the ironically named "pro-life" movement would return the United States to the condition of Chile or Colombia. And not only that, the fundamentalists try to impose the anti-life program in other countries by refusing foreign aid to programs that teach family planning, safe sex, and contraceptive knowledge. They also oppose life-saving advances through the use of stem cell research. With friends like these, "life" is in thrall to death. Carter finds these results neither loving (in religious terms) nor just (in political terms).

Carter finds the same rigid and self-righteous—and self-defeating—policies at work across the current political spectrum. The pro-life forces have no problem with a gun industry and capital punishment legislation that are, in fact, provably pro-death. Carter, a lifelong hunter, does not want to outlaw guns and he knows that Americans would never do that. But timorous politicians, cowering before the NRA, defeat even the most sensible limitations on weapons useful neither for hunting nor for personal self-defense (AK-47s, AR-15s, Uzis), even though, as Carter shows, more than 1,100 police chiefs and sheriffs told Congress that these weapons are obstacles to law enforcement. The NRA opposed background checks to keep guns out of the hands of criminals and terrorists and illegals, and then insisted that background checks, if they were imposed, had to be destroyed within twenty-four hours. The result of such pro-death measures, Carter writes, is grimly evident: "American children are sixteen times more likely than children in other industrialized nations to be murdered with a gun, eleven times more likely to commit suicide with a gun, and nine times more likely to die from firearms accidents." Where are the friends of the fetus when children are dying in such numbers?

Carter observes that "the Johns Hopkins Center for Gun Policy and Research reports that the rate of firearms homicide in the United States is *nineteen* times higher than that of 35 other high-income countries combined" (emphasis added). In the most recent year for which figures are available, these are the numbers for firearms homicides:

Ireland	54
Japan	83

Sweden	183
Great Britain	197
Australia	334
Canada	1,034
United States	*30,419*
	[emphasis added]

Once again, Carter finds no support for the policies that make such a result possible in the US, in terms of either a loving religion or a just society.

Capital punishment is also a pro-death program. It does not protect life. It aligns us with authoritarian regimes: "Ninety percent of all known executions are carried out in just four countries: China, Iran, Saudi Arabia—*and the United States*" (emphasis added). Execution does not deter, as many studies have proved. In states that abolished it, Carter writes, capital crimes did not increase:

The homicide rate is at least five times greater in the United States than in any European country, none of which authorizes the death penalty. The Southern states carry out over 80 percent of the executions but have a higher murder rate than any other region.

Texas has by far the most executions, but its homicide rate is twice that of Wisconsin, the first state to abolish the death penalty. It is not a matter of geography or ethnicity, as is indicated by similar and adjacent states: the number of capital crimes is higher, respectively, in South Dakota, Connecticut, and Virginia (all with the death sentence) than in the adjacent states of North Dakota, Massachusetts, and West Virginia (without the death penalty).

How can a loving religion or a just state support such a culture of death? Only a self-righteous and punitive fundamentalism, not an ethos of the gospels, can explain this.

It is in foreign affairs that Carter finds the most self-righteous, rigid, and self-defeating effects of a religio-political fundamentalism. It is the gap between rich and poor in the world that presents the main threat to our future, yet American policies increase that gap, at home and abroad. We give proportionally less money in foreign aid than do other developed countries, and our ability to give is being decreased by our growing deficit, incurred to reward our own wealthy families with disproportionate tax cuts. Carter points out that much of the aid announced or authorized never reaches its targets. This reflects a general smugness about America's privileged position. We are dismissive of other countries' concern with the world environment, with nuclear containment, and with international law. Carter gives specifics gathered from his world travels and from the experts' forums he regularly assembles at the Carter Center in Atlanta.

We have, for example, declared our right to first use of nuclear weapons. We have used aid money to bribe people against holding us accountable to international law. We have run secret detention centers where hundreds of people are held without formal charges or legal representation. We have rewarded with high office men who, like Alberto Gonzales, say that the Geneva Conventions on treatment of prisoners are "obsolete" or even "quaint," or who, like John Bolton, say that it is "a big mistake for us to grant any validity to international law even when it may seem in our short-term interest to do so."

The result, as Carter writes, has been to turn a vast fund of international good will accruing to us after September 11 into fear of and contempt for America unparalleled in modern times. We undermine the inspection teams of the UN and the IAEA with the result that we blunder into Iraq on bad information gathered from self-serving hacks buttering up our officialdom. On the eve of our attack on Iraq, Carter published an Op-Ed piece in *The New York Times* arguing in terms of the just war tradition that a preemptive and unilateral invasion was unjustified. Going to war was not a last resort (inspections could have continued to contain Saddam until the proof of WMDs, or the lack of them, could be established). War was not authorized by international authorities for eliminating nuclear weapons, but was an opportunity seized in order "to achieve regime change and to establish a Pax Americana in the region." It did not promise proportional violence with a clear hope of providing better conditions than the ones it was remedying. Carter's was a calm and moral judgment about the war, which most Americans now believe was the right one. In retrospect, a majority think the war was a mistake. We should have listened to Carter.

We pretend we are against nuclear proliferation, yet we spur it on when others see our disregard for the very international agreements that promote it:

> The end of America's "no first use" nuclear weapons
> policy has aroused a somewhat predictable response
> in other nations. Chinese major general Zhu Chenghu

announced in July 2005 that China's government was under internal pressure to change its "no first use" policy: "If the Americans draw their missiles and position-guided ammunition on to the target zone on China's territory, I think we will have to respond with nuclear weapons."

We attack terrorism not by cooperation with other countries' security teams, which often have better information on worldwide terrorist activities than we do, but with unilateral and preemptive uses of force that just increase terrorism. This is a new culture of death: "The US National Counter-terrorism Center," Carter writes, "reported that the number of serious international terrorist incidents more than tripled in 2004. 'Significant' attacks grew to more than 650, up from the previous record of 175 in 2003."

We claim to be spreading democracy in the Middle East, but a Zogby international poll in 2005 showed that an over-whelming majority of Arabs did not believe that US policy in Iraq was motivated by the spread of democracy in the region, and believed that the Middle East had become less democratic after the Iraq war. The approval rating of America plummeted at the very time we were supposedly bringing the blessings of freedom there—it stood, Carter notes, at "2 percent in Egypt, 4 percent in Saudi Arabia, 11 percent in Morocco, 14 percent in the United Arab Emirates, 15 percent in Jordan, with a high of only 20 percent in [our friend] Lebanon." These developments have taken place as America enacted a retreat from earlier commitments, under both Republican and Democratic presidents, that parallels what Carter describes as the retreat of evangelicals from earlier fidelity to gospel values such as life, compassion, tolerance, and inclusiveness.

Carter is a patriot. He lists all the things that Americans have to be proud of. That is why he is so concerned that we are squandering our treasures, moral even more than economic. He has come to the defense of our national values, which he finds endangered. He proves that a devout Christian does not need to be a fundamentalist or fanatic, any more than a patriotic American has to be punitive, narrow, and self-righteous. He defends the separation of church and state because he sees with nuanced precision the interactions of faith, morality, politics, and pragmatism. That is a combination that once was not rare, but is becoming more so. We need a voice from the not-so-distant past, and this quiet voice strikes just the right notes.

NOTES
1. *Our Endangered Values: America's Moral Crisis* (Simon and Schuster, 2005).
2. Juan Forero, "Latin American Women Mount Campaign to Legalize Abortion," *The New York Times*, December 3, 2005, p. A8.

**Fear and Loathing in
George W. Bush's Washington**
by Elizabeth Drew
Preface by Russell Baker

**Glory and Terror:
The Growing Nuclear Danger**
by Steven Weinberg
Preface by Anthony Lewis

Fixed Ideas: America Since 9.11
by Joan Didion
Preface by Frank Rich

*Available from your local bookseller
or at nyrb.com*

The New York Review of Books